Grown and Saved

DEDICATION

This book is dedicated to Jesus Christ, my Lord and Savior; and God the Father; and the Power of the Holy Spirit. If it was not for the Blood of the Lamb, the Grace of the Father and the Power of the Holy Spirit, I would have never become who God has created me to be.

To My Sisters and Brothers in Christ our Lord, I feel this book will encourage you to explore every possibility of your life and allow the Holy Spirit to be your ultimate guide to the true wholeness of being Grown and Saved.

To those who have yet to believe in Jesus Christ, I ask you to open your mind to the most profound experience the human mind will ever encounter.

To Mankind, take this journey with us to discover the real meaning of LOVE.

CONTENTS

4

The Beginning

Have you ever asked yourself, why was I born into this family?

- Why do I live in this house with these people?

- Why was I born a woman or man?

- Why was I born different from those around me?

- What is my purpose?
- Why was I raped?
- Why was I abused?
- Why am I not skinny?
- Why am I not beautiful?
- Why am I insecure?
- Why I am not married?
- Why did get I married?
- Why didn't God give me Children?
- Why did God give me all these Children?

- Why am I on drugs?
- Why did I have that abortion?
- Why do I love that Man or Woman?
- Why do I love the same sex?
- Why did I choose this Job?
- Why do I have these Friends?
- Why did I have and continue to have sex with these people?
- Why do I go to church?

You may have asked yourself, friends, family, and anyone else who would listen to these questions.

I have asked myself these same questions.

I have asked myself these questions because I have experienced all of these things.

I was born into a family of seven and my mother was on drugs.

I really don't know if she really understood the effect of the life she chose for herself and children.

She was escaping the pain of her past.

She raised us to the best of her ability and she was a warrior in her own stature.

As, I grew into a little girl, I found grown people interesting to study.

I wanted to know what made these people drive to either fail or succeed in life.

I would soon discover that these people would pour all of their fears, convictions, habits and beliefs into my life.

By the time I was eight years of age, I knew that the hard hustle that I saw in New York City was not all that Life had to offer.

By the time I was 11 years of age; I would experience low self-esteem and molestation and not be able to tell anyone.

So, sisters and brothers, I know how it feels to be trapped at an early age.

I would talk to myself and ask all the questions of WHY!!!!!

It is a hurtful place to be when you are trapped in a world where you have to live in fear and uncertainty of what horrors will come next.

I know all about the silent screams and how we can make our mind tell us that all things will be alright.

I know how it feels to blame yourself for the pain and disgrace for the secrets you carry.

It wasn't until years later that I would discover that all of my experiences would be for the good.

"I promised you! It will be for your Good,"

God tells us in the Word. Isaiah 44:2 reads: "Thus says the Lord who made you and formed you from the womb, who will help you."

See, I know that the pain sometimes feels unbearable and you may not know the way to go on and push forward.

But God knows how to push you forward and fight. After all, He formed you.

FIGHT, FIGHT, FIGHT! YOU WILL WIN!!!

Memories

What about the Memories of the aftershock?

Do you constantly reflect back to what could have been, what you could have done different and any of the other 'What ifs' you can think about?

I know you do because I thought about them and every person on the planet goes through the "WHAT IF MEMORIES."

These are memories that will keep us from reaching the purpose for which God created us.

"What If Memories" will allow us to move out of the situation, break up with the man or woman, get a new job, make new friends, suppress the pain, cover up the emotions, make money, get married, have children, find reglion, get off drugs, etc.,

Yet~ it is all an illusion because you never really forgot or healed from the events of the past.

I say to you, I know because it took me years to forget and heal from the events of my past.

I would act out these events in my life and exploring certain things that would cause me pain, bring pleasure and sometimes happiness, only to discover that at a certain point it would all fall apart again and again.

I would recreate myself over and over, and I am sure some of you are doing the same things.

Nothing you do really brings the peace you are craving.

Years go by and we go through several events to hopefully discover that we are living out the "WHAT IF MEMORIES."

These memories are only recurring in our life because we forget to ask God to help us remember no more.

In fact, God tells us that once we've been forgiven and blessed.

We should not remember and move on because He doesn't remember.

Isaiah 43:18: "Do not remember the former things, nor consider the things of old."

Isaiah 43:25: "I, even, I, am He who blots out your transgressions for my own sake. And I wll not remember your sins."

FORGET, FORGET AND FORGET! YOU CAN!

Forgiveness

As, we now explore the part of our soul for forgiveness in ourselves as well as other people,

I had to break the word down in my mind before I could allow it to take place in my heart.

This is a word and the processes that follows will make you become a better person if you want to or not.

Let's take a look at how this action can either bring you closer to or further you from God than you have ever been in your entire life.

The first part, 'FOR' is really for me and you to do and it belongs only to me and you.

It allows God to give us room to seek Him in His fullness.

We must go alone to the secret place and say the word 'FOR.' This will activate our minds to allow us to see what God gave for us.

Next is the word 'GIVE.' It is required to GIVE in order to RECEIVE.

See, if we give all the pain away to God and forgive the person or people that caused it in the first place, you have now opened up the door to receive the full blessing of Christ.

The last part is the, 'NESS.' It is a necessity to allow God to teach me and you how to practice FORGIVENESS in order to be joyful, peaceful, and most importantly to be complete.

It is so very important that you practice Forgiveness even when we have done nothing to receive the hurt from others.

It is a part of the Growth process for God to move in a way He can use your life.

You must learn how to process this word in your mind and then allow your heart to work.

It is God's plan for your life to open your mind and soften your heart, even in all your pain.

This is so that you will go from feeling like a victim to feeling like a conqueror that God created you to be in the first place.

You will need Forgiveness to come in first place in any situation.

Lastly, Christ practiced the ultimate Forgiveness when He gave His life for ours sins.

So let's be real. If He forgave us, why would you not forgive yourself and others?

Acts 26:18: "To open their eyes in order to turn them from darkness to light, and from the power of Satan to God, that they may receive forgiveness of sins and an inheritance among those who are sanctified by faith in Me."

FORGIVE, FORGIVE, AND FORGIVE! IT IS A MUST!

Completeness

I learned to forgive and move on and then something else appeared.

So many times as we move on and keep it moving, something will pop its head up and say, "I got you now."

You will discover that once you have craved for some type of completeness in this life, you must be very careful about what type of completeness you are in search of, because this is a journey that can trip you up very quickly.

I began taking this trip in the form of looking for attention in all the wrong places.

You may find yourself looking in a man or a woman, food, shopping, smoking, drinking, sex, lies, jobs, church hopping, pregnancies, divorces and many other forms of what we will say is completeness.

I had to learn that the only real completeness that I needed and you will also discover all you need is the completeness of God.

God has brought you through all the events of your past and present and now future.

You need to ensure that you are seeking His Completeness for your life.

You are of God's Good thing and He will complete His work in you until the last day.

2 Corinthians 13:11: "Finally, brethren, farewell. Become complete. Be of good comfort, be of one mind, live in peace, and the God of love and peace will be with you."

Philippians 1:6: "Being confident of this very thing, that He who has begun a good work in you will complete it until the day of Jesus Christ."

SEARCH FOR GOD'S COMPLETENESS. IT IS A REQUIREMENT.

Discipline

I now had to learn a word that was like speaking Greek to me.

Frankly, speaking this word will send some of you into shock.

Discipline was a part of completeness.

I know for a fact, that I was not ready for what this would mean to my life.

I am very sure that a lot of you will not to be ready for what this is going to do for your life.

See, in order to be disciplined, I would have to stand in front of the mirror and stop lying to myself about myself.

I had to keep it so real about who I was, what I wanted out of life, and the things that I was doing that I was hiding.

It also meant that I was going to have to cut people, pleasures and things off that I controlled and the control that I had on other people.

Sisters and brother's you will have to let go of control of people and things because it will eventually consume the will of God in your life.

Let it go and move into the presence of the Almighty God.

I am telling you that this is going to be the worst fight that you will have with yourself in order to experience real holiness.

God needs you to have self-discipline because of the things He is going to require of you in your life.

You must bring your will in line with God's Will or it will never work.

I figured out that, without discipline, all my dreams and desires would truly be lost and God could not move on my behalf.

God can't move if you have no discipline; and if God doesn't move, you will end up in poverty and shame.

I know for myself that discipline didn't come easy but it was God's love for me that kept me in all of His Grace.

I pray that you will be willing to find God's discipline for your life.

Proverbs 15:10: "Harsh discipline is for him who forsakes the way and he who hates correction will die."

DISCIPLINE, DISCIPLINE, DISCIPLINE! IT WILL SAVE YOUR LIFE!

Defilements

I prepare to explore the word defilements; I will need to be very careful on how I express my view on this word to you.

This word comes in so many forms in our lives that I may not be able to cover it all.

But here we go.

I have discovered that defilement comes in many disguises.

It may come in the form of our mouth, attitudes, and conditions of our hearts, actions, beliefs and morals.

However, it shows up, if you don't recognize it, you can count on the fact that it will keep you from discovering the real you.

Defilement showed up in my life in the form of my mouth.

That's right, the mouth and the way I use my tongue as a double-edged sword.

This form is the most deadly because it governs our thought process and our actions definitely come along for the fun.

I would say and do things that were untamable.

I would use my mouth and tongue to build and destroy all in the same breath.

I wonder how many of you do the same thing.

I learned how to use my mouthpiece at an early age and it came naturally at that point.

I studied adults and acted out the things they would say in my presence.

I would see the ones who were in the church, praise, gossip, speak of love and empowerment and then cut their neighbor and families down with the same tongue.

Next, I saw the ones in the street doing the same thing.

So I figured, this is what you do whether you knew Jesus or not.

By the time I was eight years of age, I could curse like a sailor and it was fun.

I would use my mouth to get whatever I wanted or needed.

Next, let's talk about the actions that came with the mouth.

I would fight, love, corrupt, praise and gossip all with the same tongue.

I would later discover that this mouth would almost cost me my life and salvation,

After, years of ups and downs because of my mouth and actions, I found myself broken-hearted, not willing to trust and, worst of all, trapped in my own world that landed me on a fast track to hell.

See, once again, I had to go to the mirror and point the finger.

I know that many of you are on the same track.

I had to go and find out what God and the Scriptures had to say about my mouth, tongue and actions.

I went to God in all my mess in the middle of my living room floor and asked for the ultimate help.

I wanted to live and not die!

I know that you to want to live and not perish.

You may not have the same defilement I had, but at some point in time in your life you will be faced with yours.

I pray you ask God for help with it in whatever form it shows up.

Remember that the power of Life and Death is in the tongue.

Proverbs 21:23: "Whoever guards his mouth and tongue keeps his soul from troubles."

THE POWER OF THE TONGUE IS REAL. SO BE CLEAR ON THE THINGS YOU USE IT FOR.

Deeds

We have now reached a point where I speak to each of you about your deeds you are issuing out in your life.

It is amazing how women, men and children do not understand that what they do to other people will and shall come back to their lives.

See, before I was saved by the blood of the Lamb, I was one of those women who would think that I would not have to answer for the dirt and the ugliness I was doing in other people's lives.

Some of you at this point may say, "I never do anything to anybody" or "I keep getting hurt because I trust too much or love to hard. I try to help everyone I meet.'

I used to say all of this myself until I discovered that I was causing disappointment to the one who wanted the best out of my deeds: God.

God wants all your deeds to be done in Spirit and in Truth.

How many of us can say that we really did all of our deeds in Spirit and in Truth?

Think about it, I will wait. Time is up.

Sisters, brothers and children, we have been getting something out of the deal the whole time.

We all know that most of the time we either help because we want people to be pleased with our actions or we want a desire to be fulfilled.

I had to learn the way you will learn that our deeds are to better someone else; it is not just about you.

IT'S NOT ABOUT YOU! Your deeds are a reflection of how God wants you to help and give to other people.

Deeds are assignments from God to help someone with their salvation.

It is not to support them financially. It is not to carry them emotionally.

It is not to determine what you think they should do with their life. It is all so God can get the Glory and allow us to become the best people God wants us to be.

Please don't misunderstand!

I'm not saying don't contribute to help or aiding God's people.

Just make sure you check that the deed is what God wants for you and the people involved.

Deeds are also a future investment when you may need to make a withdrawal from the ultimate power, Jesus.

He will carry you!

So run and ask God and the power of the Holy Spirit if the deeds you currently have on the books are pleasing in the sight of the Lord.

It takes practice so be patient and always ask if a deed is going to help with my salvation and the salvation of someone else.

Proverbs 20:11: "Even a child is known by his deeds, whether what he does is pure and right."

DEEDS. LET THEM BE DONE IN SPIRIT AND IN TRUTH.

Backslider

I received all this knowledge, I was ready to save so many lives and help so many people.

I thought I had it all together because God had given revelation after revelation and I was worshipping, raising my children, working and just living the newfound Holy Spirit-filled life.

This probably sounds like some of you; and if not you, just wait, the test is on the way.

So many times after we are saved as humans, we will focus on all the new things God is doing in our lives but what about all the old things that were so much fun?

I had to experience some real backsliding stuff to write about it.

Sisters and brothers, I tell you Satan showed up so good looking, smelling good, with money, and he knew the Word of God. I thought for sure I had hit a diamond mine.

But little did I know that this was a snake-filled lie from the enemy camp to destroy me and it almost did take a sister right out of the Will of God.

I thank God for His Son Jesus who was interceding all the time on my behalf.

I will begin by telling you that, when you get a new thing going on, you have to ask for the power of the Holy Spirit to give you certain gifts to help you along the walk.

I was a single mother of four sons at the time and I was putting my self back through school to start a new career.

Satan took my weakness and used it against me.

I was used to having a man in my life. Whether he was a good man or bad man, if he was of the male species he was in my life.

My thought process was I could help him and he could help me and ease some of the loneliness

Then, the test appeared!

I thought this man was what I needed. See, I didn't meet this brother in a nightclub or sports bar. He spotted me doing what I must do, shop for my sons.

As I got to know this man, I grew to admire him. He knew the Word of God and spoke it so promisingly.

I let my sons get to know him as well. But as time progressed, I noticed that I was beginning to look like and do things like the old me.

I found us having sex, smoking, clubbing, and dealing with people and thoughts I had left behind.

Oh, don't think he didn't go to church with me and the children because he did. Like I said, he knew the Word.

As time passed, I felt the connection of God slowly getting silent.

God was weeping at the fact that I was doing what so many **CHRISTIAN WOMEN/MEN** are doing: **BACKSLIDING** while trying to justify their actions by saying, 'God knows my heart and I'm not perfect.'

WOW! Does this look like some of you? Get the mirror, because it just might be you.

I had to come to a decision and a very hard one I must add.

I finally told him that I had to stop using the drugs, clubbing and sexing him because I needed for him to love me enough to marry me.

That's when his true self showed up. Remember, Satan will always show you who he is and what you mean to him.

You discover that you mean nothing to Satan or the vessels he uses to steal you back from God.

After, the relationship ended and I was full of guilt and shame, Jesus came to me in my room and told me that he was married to me and that he loved me more than any earthly man could love me.

He showed me through Scriptures that I was made clean again and He wanted me more than ever to do His will.

Jesus taught me, through the power of the Holy Spirit, how to fight and respect myself.

He wiped the guilt away from me and took the Spirit of Rejection from me.

Your backsliding may not be in the form of the need for a man or woman but there might be something in your secret closet.

I pray that you will please allow God to work you through your backsliding experience and allow the Holy Spirit to flow through you.

Jeremiah 3:14: "Return O' backsliding children says the Lord: For I am married to you. I will take you, one from a city and two from family, and I will bring you to Zion. And I will give you shepherds according to MY heart who will feed you with knowledge and understanding."

RETURN FROM YOUR BACKSLIDING AND BE FREED FROM THE GUILT AND PAIN, FOR HE LOVES YOU MORE THAN YOU CAN UNDERSTAND!!!!!!

Awakening

I was wiped clean by the BLOOD OF CHRIST.

He renewed my mind, soul and spirit; I felt an overwhelming feeling of a certain type of awakening.

I could see clearer and hear clearer than I could ever do before in life.

See, sisters and brothers, when God, the Holy Spirit and Jesus Christ renew your life, you are changed forever.

Things begin to take a different turn and people will begin to notice the change as well.

I need to tell you that Satan also knows that you have been cleaned and washed in the Blood of Christ.

The enemy will begin to try to create situations that may make you think that things are getting worse or not moving fast, but this is a trick!

Please stay focused and don't look at what you see but trust the new awakening inside of you that is now talking to you and working on your behalf in every aspect of your life.

You must trust that God wants the best for your life!

The awakening is also a process that may make you feel like you are an alien and in this all alone.

This is not the situation and God is beginning to have an intimate relationship with you and wants you all to Himself.

He will show you how much He loves you and wants to teach you His ways.

Please don't be surprised that the old people you were socializing or had friendships with prior to the awakening begins to tell you that you are different and acting different.

This is exactly what you want to hear because it confirms the one thing God loves and that is spiritual growth in Him.

My awakening was the greatest thing that could have ever happened to me.

I was on my way to a real intimate love affair with my Lord and Savior Jesus Christ.

I pray that you will be able to embrace your awakening. It is needed and required in order for God to complete His work in you.

1 Corinthians 15:34: "Awake to righteousness and sin not for some of the knowledge of God."

AWAKE, AWAKE, AWAKE AND ALLOW THE LORD OF THE HEAVENS AND EARTH TO FILL YOU WITH THE POWER!!!!!!

Calling

The calling came as a surprise to me. After I embraced the awakening that God had to offer.

He started to download and give me memos of the assignments He wanted me to take.

I thought all God wanted me to do was tell people about Him and His life every now and then.

I was in left field and so many of you are in left field as well. God wanted ME to work for Him 24 hours a day, 7 days a week, and 365 days a year.

When I got the call to go to work, I was doing just fine.

See, I changed my habits, started going to church on normal routine, and began teaching my children and some friends who would believe me.

I was living and loving life, moving in the right direction.

When, God dropped the word on me and asked me if I was willing to die for Him.

I tell you the truth, just when I figured it was all working out.

God came and asked for something I thought I was free from, which was dying.

I know that some of you are feeling that way too, like "God, I thought I was doing enough to please you.

Now, you want more of me and I really like the way things are going because it is definitely better than that hell I was living before I found you."

I know how you are feeling because I felt that same way.

I told God, "I am just learning how to live and now you want me to die."

I said, "God, who is going to listen to me anyway!

I have been a dope user, stripper, dealer, woman of the night and had other women being women of the night, abused by men that I loved and now I was this single parent of four small boys trying to make a dollar out of 15 cents."

I finally had found some answers and now God stepped the process up on me.

I didn't answer God and I continued to do what I wanted to do.

That is when He honored me with another visit that changed the course of my destiny forever.

As I stood in my room in the mirror, He spoke to me and said, "Daughter, if you don't die for Me, you will die without Me."

At that very moment, I broke down as if I was having a nervous breakdown. My Beloved God told me that I would be without Him.

All the changing and doing the right thing could not help me with true salvation if I was not willing to do what He required of me.

I said, YES to my assignments for I knew that obedience was better than sacrifice.

God told me to go and teach the Word of God and not to compromise God's principles ever again in my life.

Some of you are ignoring God's call on your life and think that He will understand on the Day of Judgment.

Beloved, He won't.

He wants obedience from each of us to do His work in this earth and He is calling His people who are listening for His voice to do His will.

You may say, "She doesn't know what she is writing about."

God loves me and He will understand if I remain in this place where I am comfortable."

No! He requires that you have faith to go to the new place He has called you.

It is impossible to please God without Faith.

Faith equals obedience; they are one and the same.

I pray that you will answer the call that God has put on your life and you will explore Faith and Obedience.

John 15:16: "You have not chosen me, but I have chosen you, and ordained you, that you should go and bring forth fruit that your fruit should remain; that whatsoever you shall ask of the Father in my name, He may give it you."

Isaiah 66:4: "I also will choose their delusions, and will bring their fears upon them; because when I called, none did answer; when I spoke, they did not hear; but they did evil before thy eyes, and chose that in which I delighted not."

ANSWER THE CALL. HE IS WAITING AND GOD DOESN'T DO CALL WAITING!

Nakedness

I accepted the calling and started walking in Faith and Obedience;

I realized that I was truly unaware of what this truly meant.

Some of you are wearing those same shoes right now in your life.

This particular walk could not be done by simply studying the Bible, doing good things and cutting off some people from my past.

It really did mean that I would have to get nude in front of the Lord.

Some of you are saying at this point, "What in the world is she speaking of, getting NUDE before the Lord?"

This means that you have to put everything in the open, all the ugly and pretty and any in between that may come up along the way.

I had to go all the way back to my insecurities and generational family ties and bring this before the Lord.

For a sister like me and some of you, this is a very unpleasant place.

I had to place in front of the Lord, Jesus and Holy Spirit all the morals, beliefs and concepts

I had been raised up on and developed along the way as a woman.

I had to talk with God about my body, goals, dreams, fears, misconceptions, men, sex, and everything that God told me to hand over to Him that He may wipe away.

I have come to understand that getting nude in front of the Lord means that we must merely go to Him the way we go to a best friend, parents, spouses, lovers, therapists, or anyone I felt comfortable talking over my private matters.

I know that God will show each of you a way to come before Him and be completely nude with Him.

I pray that God will whisper in your ear to come to Him and release and discuss everything that affects you.

Isaiah 41:13: "For I, Lord your God, will hold your right hand saying to you, and Fear not, I will help you."

GET NUDE BEFORE THE LORD YOUR GOD. IT IS THE PLACE TO BE!

New Experience

There comes a time in a person's life when they have done all they can do and loved and trusted people as much as they could possible trust. Then, they are faced with the "DOOR".

The door is the place where we feel we have learned our life lessons and have given all we can, yet still we come up short.

It is a place where you still find yourself wanting and desiring more out of your life.

It seems that the more you try, the more it appears that things around you feel totally out of sort.

The people you thought had your back and would stand with you in the midst of all your troubles somehow now appear to be a little on the breezy side.

This is the point where I had to figure out that Jesus was telling me that He is the Door. The Door is Jesus.

So many times, we keep asking for the opportunity and/or a certain someone to make things better to add value to our life.

Yet, when the things don't show up fast enough or we lose patience with the wait.

We wonder what we will do next to move into the destiny that awaits us.

It is time to walk to the DOOR and let Him guide you and me to the next level of the great unknown.

Jesus knows the voice of His sheep and lambs and will guide you in all things.

Put your hand and plans in the hand of the Master planner who is the author and finisher of your life.

Let the Power of the Holy Spirit flow so free in your life.

John 10:7: "Most assuredly, I say to you. I am the door of the sheep."

PLEASE RUN TO THE DOOR. HE AWAITS YOU!

ENCOURAGE YOURSELF

LOVE

HOPE

FAITH

WISDOM

Restored

Now that I have found the DOOR and you have found the DOOR, it is time for us to talk about what it means to be restored.

This word and the meaning of this word should and will take on a new meaning to you.

See, I once thought the word meant to get something back that was once taken from me.

I am sure that some of you thought or still think of this word in that manner.

As I became closer to Christ, I discovered the real meaning of this word. I was amazed that it didn't mean to get something back.

In Christ, it means to give us something brand new.

How many times do we want something new, whether it is a new church, job, man, house, life, furniture or mindset?

We search the world trying to figure out how to get what we want but it is not until you allow God to restore to you do you truly understand that Christ makes you new.

He has to make you new again because the old you would never be satisfied with what Christ gives you because the old you would keep battling for the old things or the old experiences with Christ.

Beloved, when Christ restores to you, it is all the missing ingredients that you didn't have before.

The old you must die. It can no longer live with the new you in the new experience.

Good and pure can't live with old and nasty.

Light and darkness can't live together.

See, in the end, it doesn't matter what way I say it.

The new positive you can't and won't put up with the old negative you or the old experiences with Christ.

So please accept it and be restored.

Luke 5:37-38: "And no one puts new wine into old wineskins. Otherwise, the skins burst, the wine spills out, and the skins are ruined. But they put new wine into fresh wineskins, and both are preserved."

THE LORD HAS AND WILL RESTORE YOU. ALLOW YOURSELF TO BECOME BRAND NEW!

Struggles

The brand new you and I are in place and things are moving in a positive direction and we still feel this heavenly high of peace—and then out of the blue we are hit by this one word that changes everything.

This thing rears its ugly head and throws us off our game of peace and restoration.

This thing called struggle shows itself.

Struggle this time seems as if it is hitting us with the power and force of the universe behind it.

In all actualities, it is the universes coming at us because now Satan and his forces are aware of the new you and the new experience you have had with Christ.

Satan and his forces are going to use you against yourself and anything Satan thinks will make you turn from God.

The Bible shares and is full of God's people and how they dealt with struggles.

You must remind yourself during these times that "I AM GOD'S SERVANT, AND HE TAKES PLEASURE IN MY PROSPERITY".

Jesus want nothing more than to give you joy.

Whatever you need at this time ask for the guidance from the Holy Spirit to led you into all truth.

We do have a new immune system when Jesus takes over, but it is to help us understand that we are more than conquerors and we have victory.

Those of us who have not had the privilege to encounter this, it is called the Flesh against the Spirit and the Spirit against the Flesh.

This means that your human nature is now in battle with your spirit nature.

Your flesh is described as the ways in which the human nature operates.

For example, if someone hurts you, the human nature wants you to respond by hurting someone back by being evil.

If finances become a problem, and you stop praying and give in to what the Devil has to say.

If we act on our human nature, then Satan and his forces are allowed once again to come into your mind, body, spirit and soul.

If we flee into the arms of Jesus and admit to Him that your heart is heavy and your spirit is getting weak.

The great instructor (Holy Spirit) will then tell you that He knew this would come but you are in me and I am in you. I will fight for you.

It can be extremely hard to stay in the Spirit and live in the Spirit.

I have learned that we can't just say we walk with Jesus.

We must live with Jesus!

I tell you to please live in Jesus in all ways so that He may live in you and keep you in his arms.

He foretold us that this would come through Apostle Paul. So if he sent word, then you know He (Jesus) has the only answer.

Galatians 5:17: "For the **flesh** lusts **against** the **Spirit** and the **Spirit against** the **flesh**; and these are **contrary** to one another, so that **you do not do** the things that you wish."

THE LORD WILL KEEP YOU IN ALL YOUR WAYS through all your struggles!

Treasures

In this section, we will discover God's treasures. What are treasures? The treasures that will be explored will not be the treasures of jewels but the treasures of Life. Your life treasures will bring into your life all of your heart's desires.

So many times we do not recognize that we are the biggest and greatest treasure because the world has told us that all the important things are in collecting and gathering cars, degrees, money, careers, and the list could continue.

However, after we have gone through life collecting and gathering these things, we still find ourselves without the necessary treasures to get us through what money, relationships, marriage, careers, homes, relocation, divorce, childbirth, churches, pastors, social organization and anything else we could become a part of trying to fix the void that still remains in the heart.

When I asked the Holy Spirit to guide me to write this section, the Power of the Lord said to me to tell you that the following treasures are the answers to your tears and the up's and down's of your emotions:

- Knowledge—not man's knowledge but God's Knowledge

- Wisdom of God~ not man's wisdom but divine wisdom from God

- Understanding—in God's way, which will give you understanding of man's ways

- Revelation—the process that allows the Father to give you insight from Heaven

- Confidence—the process of knowing and being sure of yourself in a Godly way

- Generosity—giving to God and to others

- Humility—to give your heart over to God and humble yourself

- Faith~~ to believe the impossible

- Discerning of Spirits~ divine ability to see a spirit that motivates human being if good or bad

- Peace~ Not as Man give you peace but peace that Jesus gives that surpasses all understanding

- Love~ the abundance of the heart that has divine flow and heals all the woes of the world

- Attitude—the process of having positive reactions in letting the Power of God make you over

The Apostle's Note

I will like to send love to everyone who is reading this book. This book is so special because it is my testimony of how God save me for such a time as this.

To my son's you little people are the reason I am in my right mind to do the will of the Lord. You guys saved mommy's life. Thank you all.

To my Husband you are my love and air. I thank God for your hand in marriage.

To my family and friends thank you all for praying.

Made in the USA
Columbia, SC
28 August 2019